VOWEL
TABLE OF CO

VOWELS

Reading is an exciting challenge for the first grade child. While eager to learn the necessary skills, the path along the way can be intimidating. The pages in this book, *Vowels*, are designed to provide the necessary skill practice of associating letters and the sounds they stand for in a fun, friendly way. Tongue twisters introduce the long and short vowel sounds. Tongue twisters are not only fun, but they encourage verbal skills and an appreciation for the written language. Children also practice writing these letters while reinforcing the sounds.

ORGANIZATION

Children first learn the short vowels and the sounds they stand for. They then learn the long vowel sounds and the letter combinations which represent them. The letters are not introduced in alphabetical order. Some vowel sounds are easier for children to distinguish than others, so they are taught first in this book.

For each vowel sound, children first learn the letter-sound association. A key picture at the top of the page reminds students of the vowel sound. The picture may not follow the same rule that is reinforced on the page. Students practice writing the capital and lower forms as a review of letter recognition. They then quickly progress to identifying pictures whose names contain the vowel sounds. Students also identify letter sounds and blend them to say words. Finally, they combine all the skills to read simple sentences in which the words repeat the vowel sound.

USE

The pages in this book are designed as practice for letter-sound association. After sharing the corresponding tongue twister, copies of the activities can be given to individuals, pairs of students, or small groups for completion. Copies of the tongue twisters can be made and sent home with children if you are using the activities as additional home practice.

To begin, determine the implementation which best fits your students' needs and your classroom structure. The following plan is a suggested format.

- **Introduce:** Tell children they will learn about a new letter and the sound it stands for. Explain that you will read a tongue twister which repeats a vowel sound. Encourage them to listen carefully for the repeated sound. After children identify the sound, write the letter on the board and explain which vowel sound, long or short, the tongue twister represents. Challenge children to practice saying the sentence several times, increasing the speed each time.

- **Worksheet:** Show children a copy of the activity page. Repeat the tongue twister and point out the key picture. Have students trace the solid letters with a finger while repeating the consonant's sound. Let children know that the activities on the page will be fun as well as helpful. Explain the skill and how they are to complete the page.

- **Follow-up:** Repeat the tongue twister and point out the key picture. Review the page with children. Work with students having difficulty by providing additional practice sheets.

ADDITIONAL IDEAS

- **Parent Letter:** Send the *Letter to Parents* home with children. The letter explains the ways parents can help their child.

- **Assessment Test:** On pages 4 and 5, you will find an assessment test; one page assesses short vowel sounds and the other assesses long vowel sounds. You can use the test as a diagnostic tool by administering it before children begin the activities in this book. After children have completed the workbook, let them retake the test to gauge the progress they have made.

- **Individual Observation Checklist:** The checklist is a recording device to help maintain a master list of individual student progress. As you observe each student's completion of a task, check it on the list. You may wish to place the completed checklist in each student's portfolio or send it home with additional activity sheets for the child needing further skill practice.

- **Tongue Twisters:** Tongue twisters using each long and short vowel sound are included on page 62. They are grouped by short and long vowels, then listed alphabetically. There are several ways to use these pages. You could enlarge copies of the selected tongue twister for each student. While not able to read all the words, students can begin to associate reading with printed words on the page. Children can also take the tongue twisters home to parents to encourage reading at home as well as to reinforce the identified vowel and the sound it represents.

- **Answer Key:** Answers for each activity page are listed on pages 63 and 64.

- **Extending Learning:** Invite students to draw a picture illustrating the tongue twister. They might even enjoy writing their own tongue twister or silly sentence to further reinforce each vowel sound. After students share their tongue twisters, collect them and bind them to make a class book representing each vowel. Place the book in the class library.

- **Bulletin Board:** Display completed worksheets on a bulletin board to show student progress. Pictures illustrating the tongue twisters could also be displayed with a copy of the sentence.

Name ______________________________

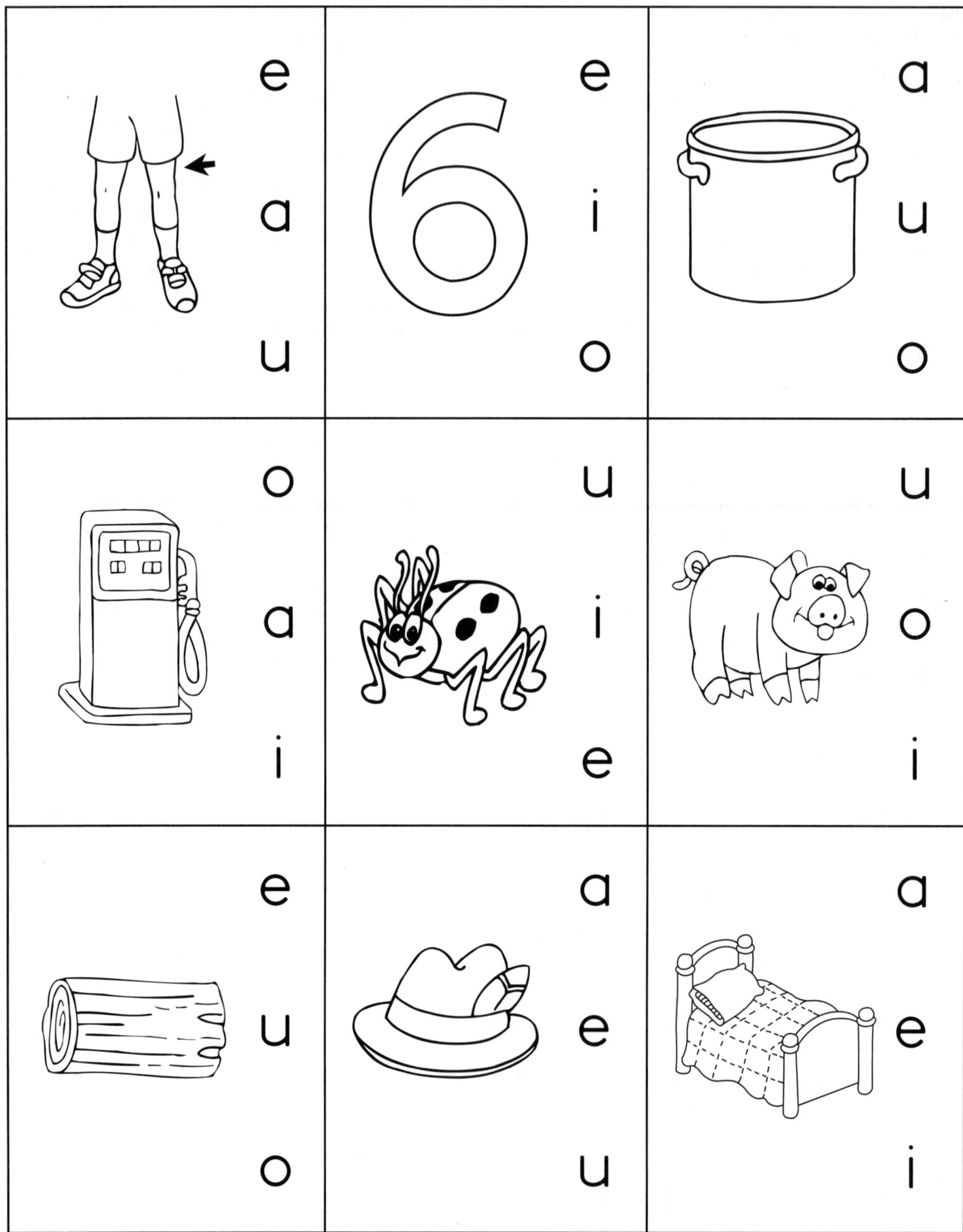

Assessment: Short Vowel Sounds Circle the letter that stands for the vowel sound in each picture name.

Name ______________________________

Assessment: Long Vowel Sounds Circle the letter that stands for the vowel sound in each picture name.

INDIVIDUAL OBSERVATION CHECKLIST

Name ______________________________

Vowel	Identifies Short Sound	Identifies Long Sound	Writes Capital	Writes Lower Form
a				
e				
i				
o				
u				

Dear Parents,

Phonics teaches the relationship between letters and the sounds they represent. It is an essential element to any reading program. However, learning this association can be intimidating for children. Vowels are especially challenging since each letter can make a variety of sounds.

As your child learns the vowels and the sounds they represent, you can help your child at home in many ways. Together, review completed activity sheets your child brings home. Ask your child to explain the page. This discussion often reinforces the information children learn in class. Also, play letter games with words on food products, street signs, and written materials. For example, point out a vowel letter in a one syllable word and ask your child to say its name. After saying the word, have your child identify if they hear a short or long vowel sound. Then help your child think of other words that contain that vowel sound. Encourage your child to use the words to make up silly sentences. (For example: The sheep speaks to the queen about peaches and peas.)

From time to time, I may send home activity sheets. To best help your child, please consider the following suggestions:

- Provide a quiet work place.
- Go over the directions together.
- Encourage your child to do his or her best.
- Together, check the lesson. Note improvements as well as problems.

Thank you for your help. Your encouragement and support are an integral part of your child's learning process.

Sincerely,

Name

Aa

ant

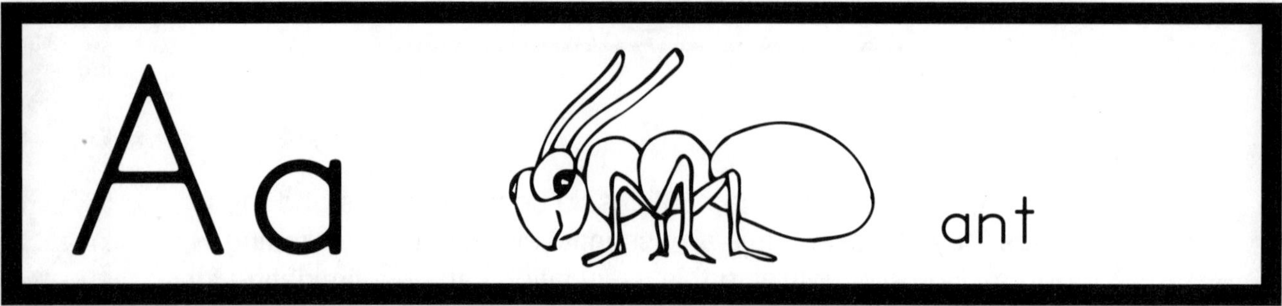

Aa

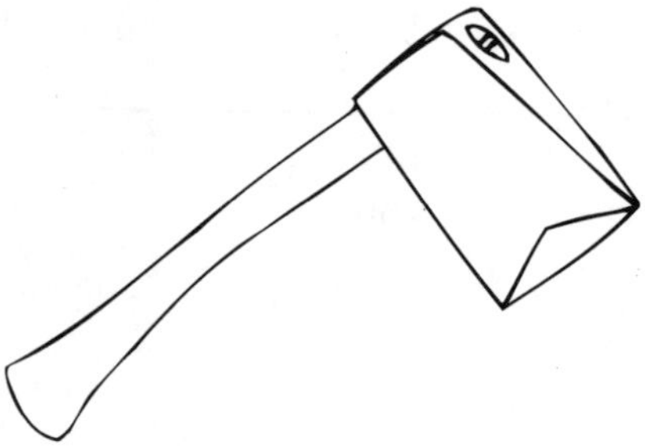

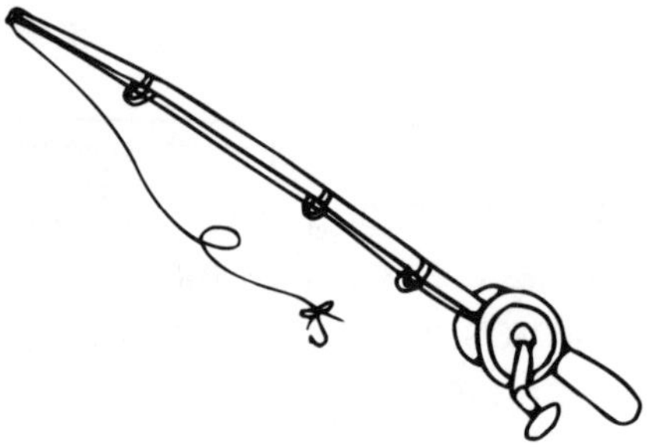

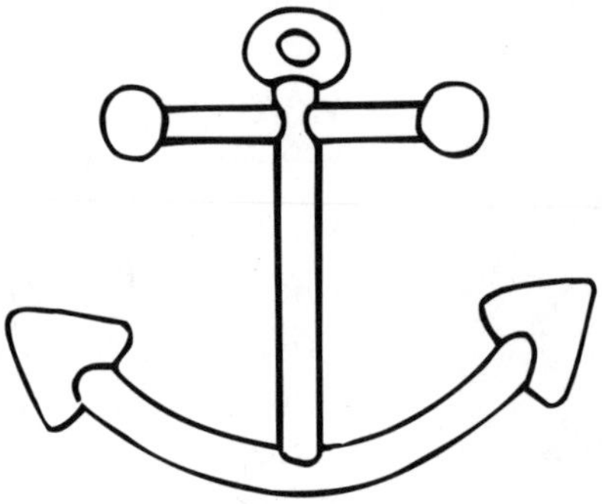

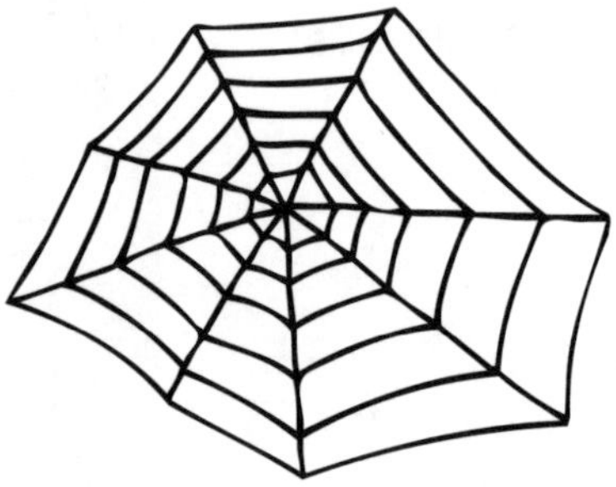

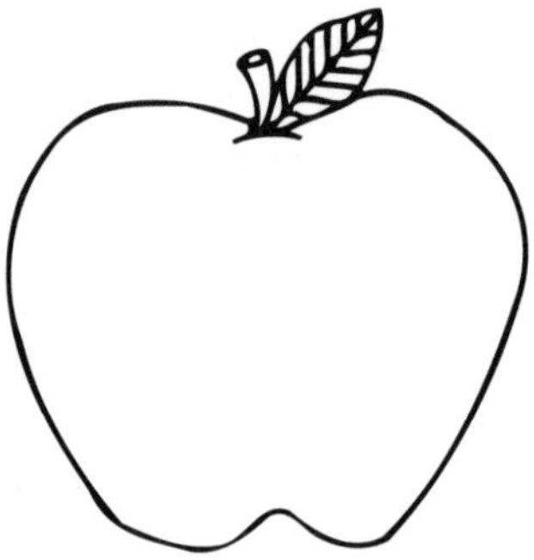

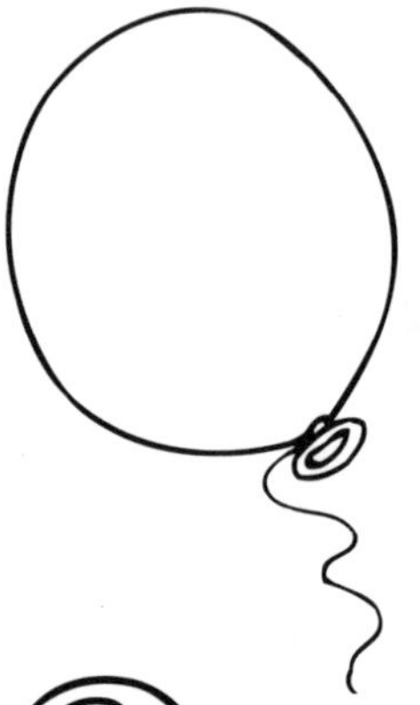

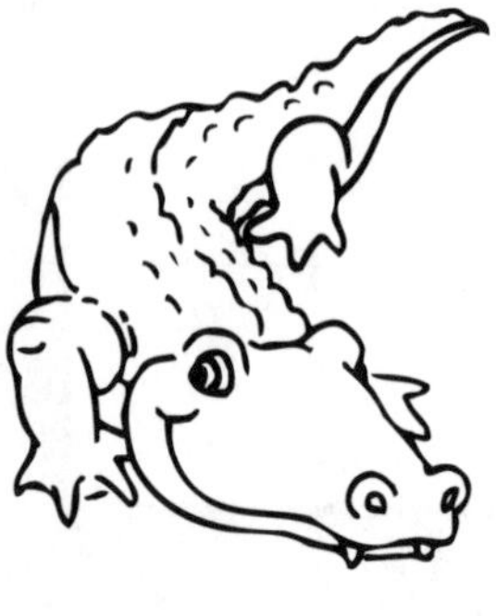

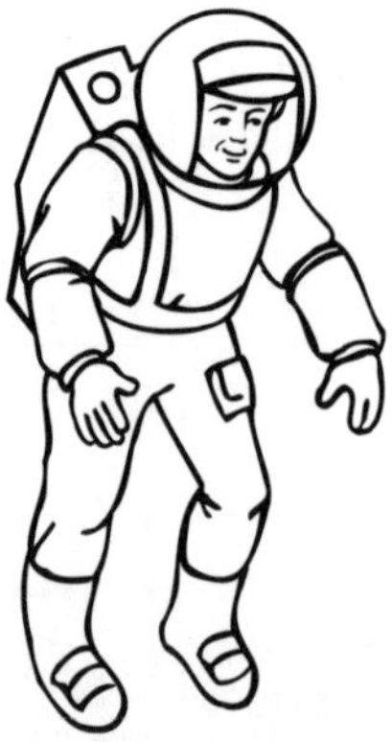

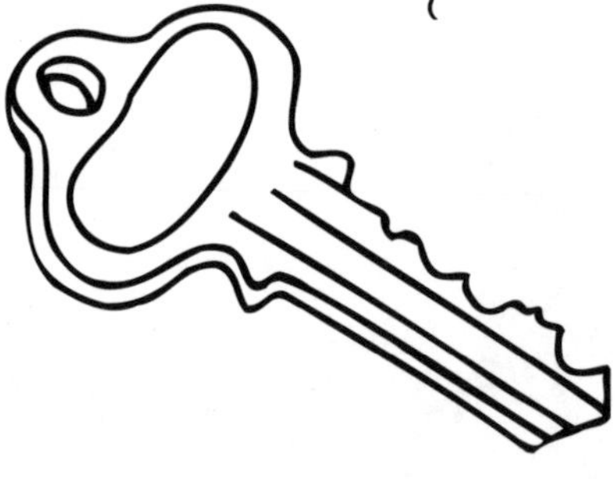

Initial Short a Trace and write the letters. Color the pictures whose names begin with the short *a* sound.

Name ______________________

a cap

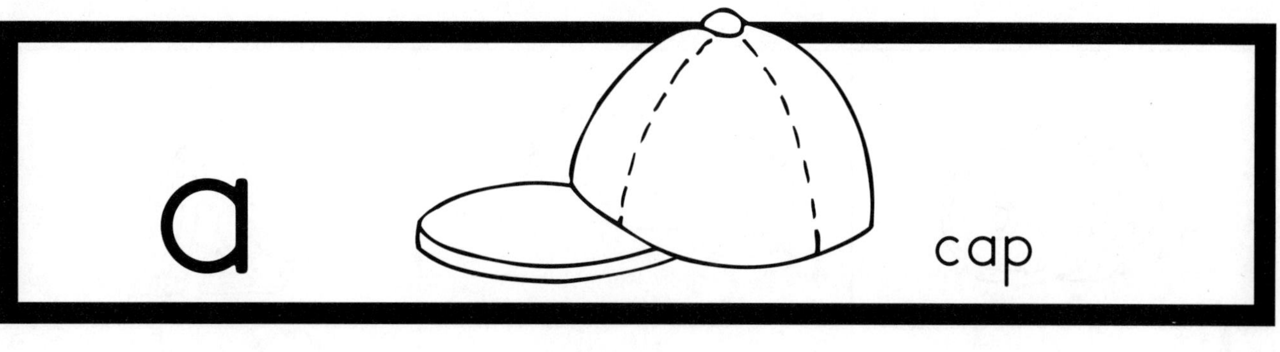

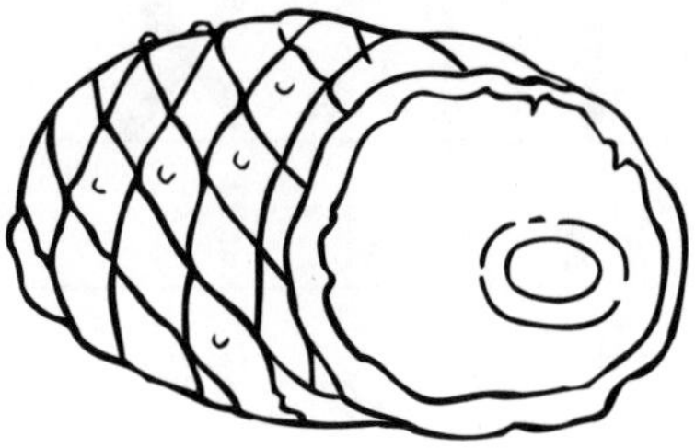
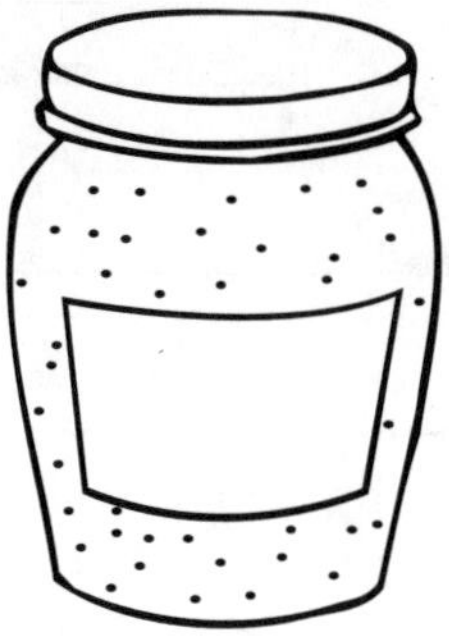
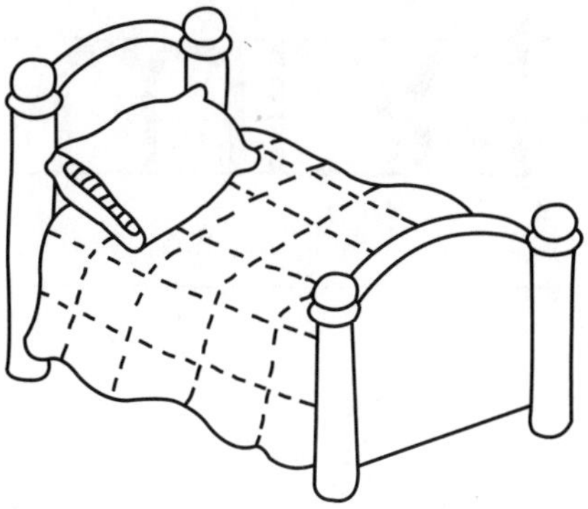
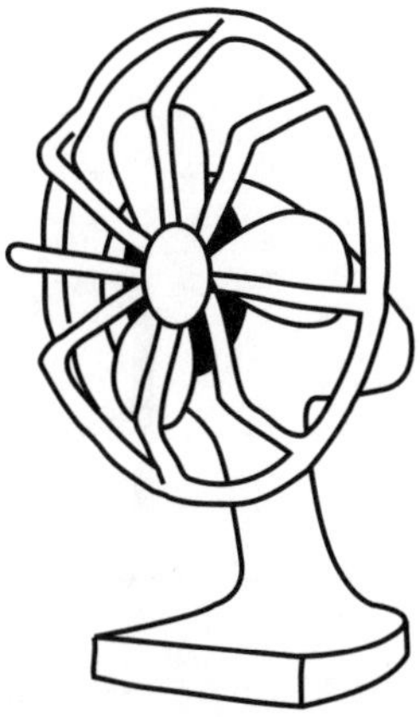
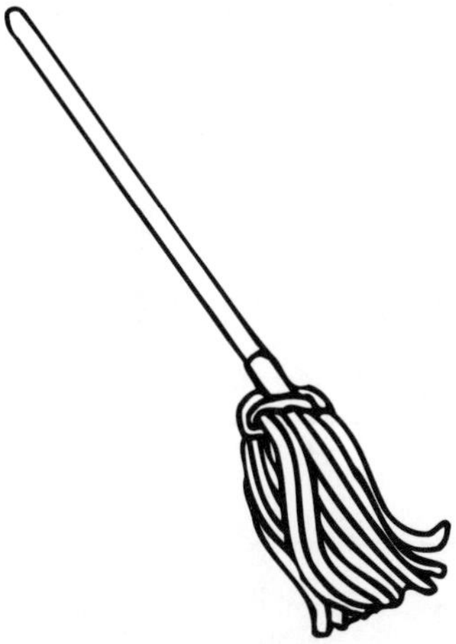
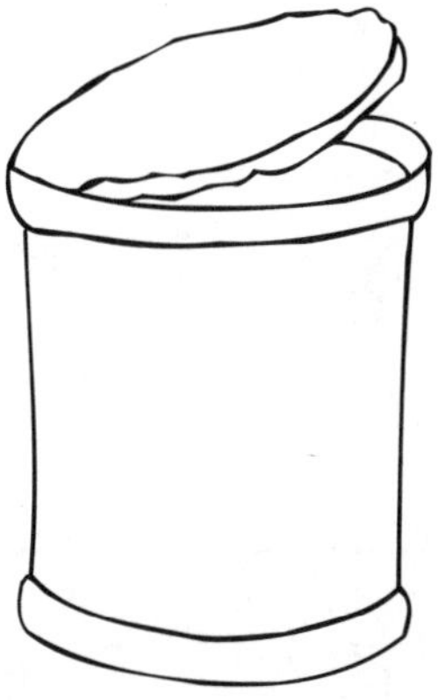
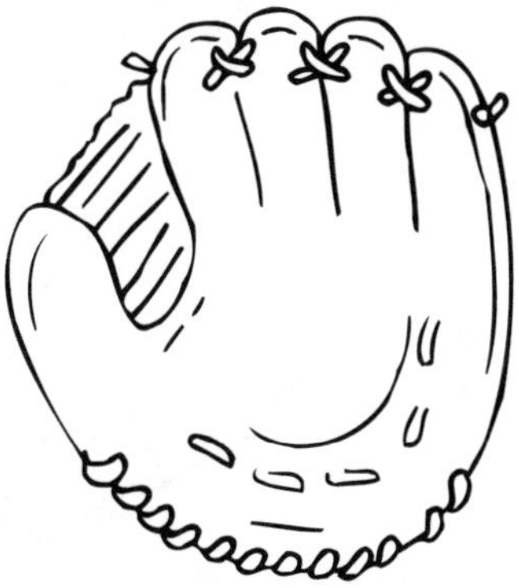
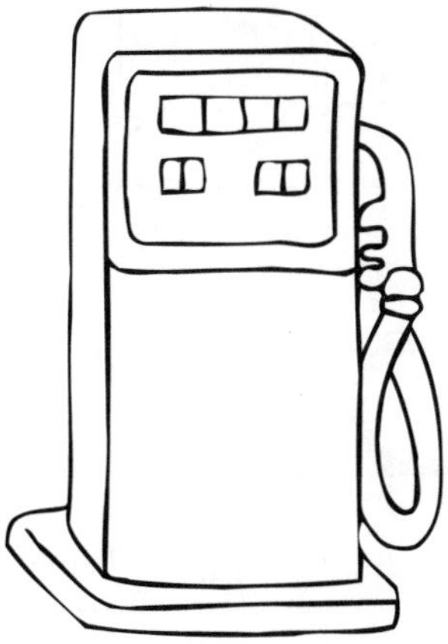
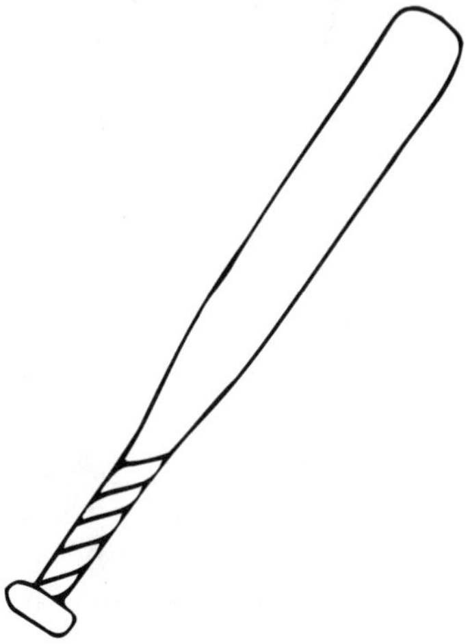

Medial Short a Color the pictures whose names have the short *a* sound.

Name

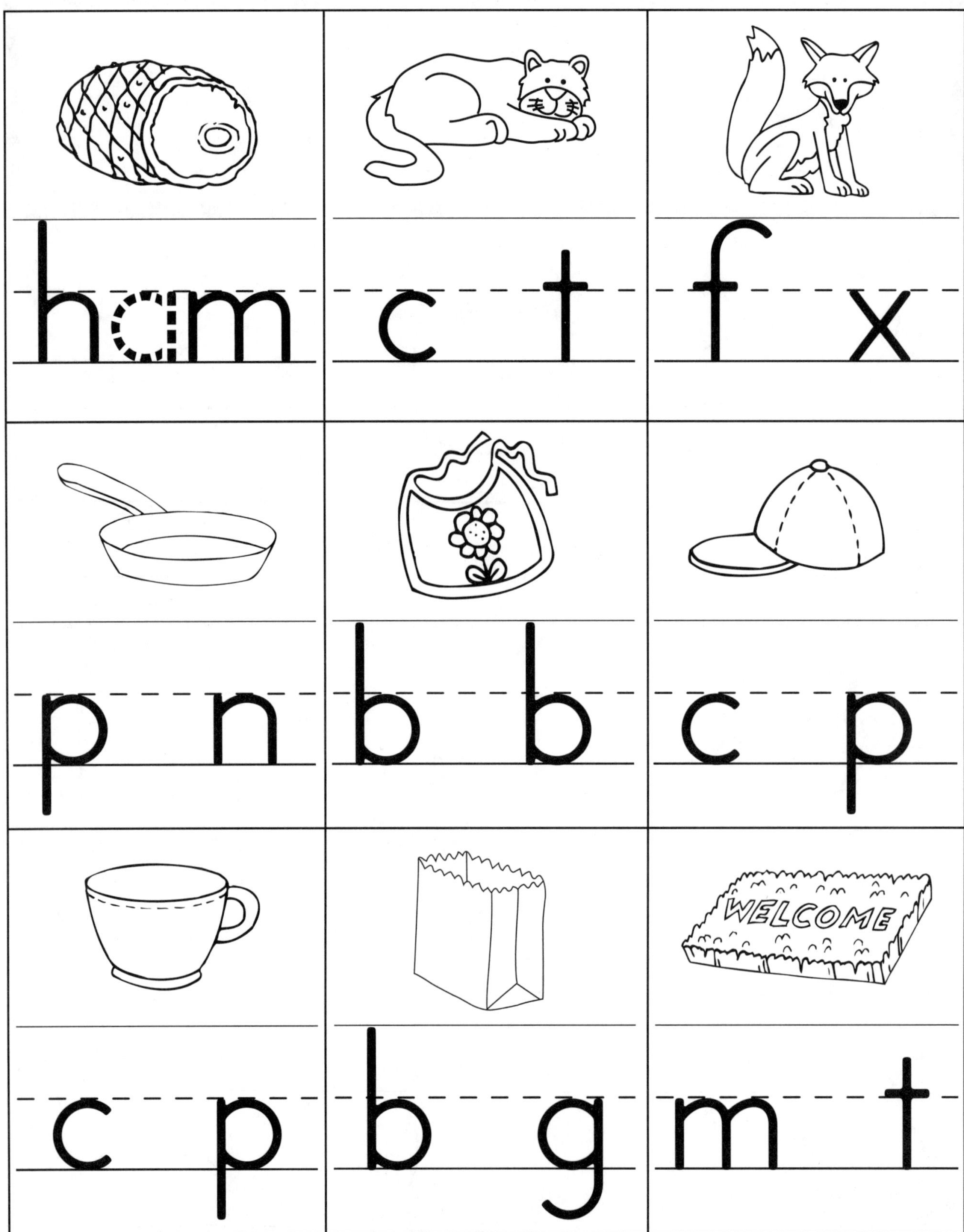

Completing Short a Words Write *a* to complete each word whose name has the short *a* sound.

Name

p

a

n

tag bag lap

ham jam ran

mat map tag

fan tap fat

had ham hat

Recognizing Short a Words Blend and write the first word. Then circle the word that names each picture, and write it on the line.

Name

The cat is in the ________.

bag pan

The hat is on the ________.

tag man

Jam is on the ________.

map can

The fan is on the ________.

cap ham

Completing Short a Sentences Write the word on the line that completes each sentence.

Name

O o

octopus

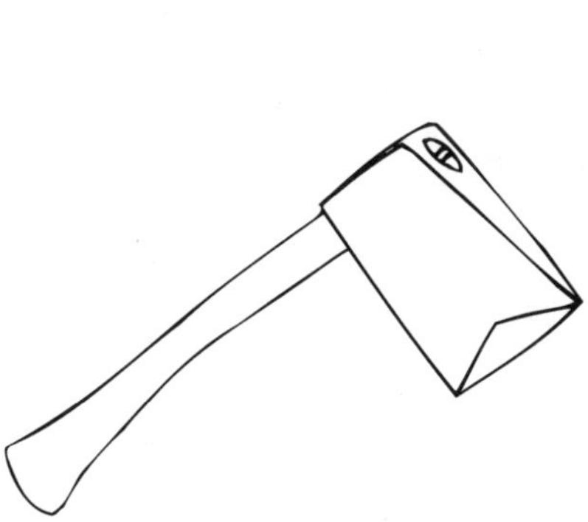

Initial Short o   Trace and write the letters. Color the pictures whose names begin with the short *o* sound.

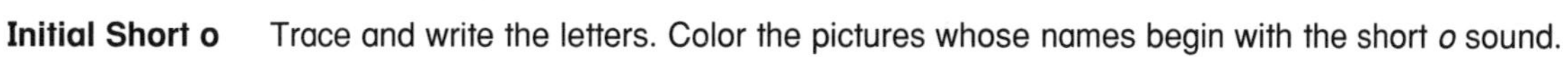

Name ______________________

Medial Short o Color the pictures whose names have the short *o* sound.

Name

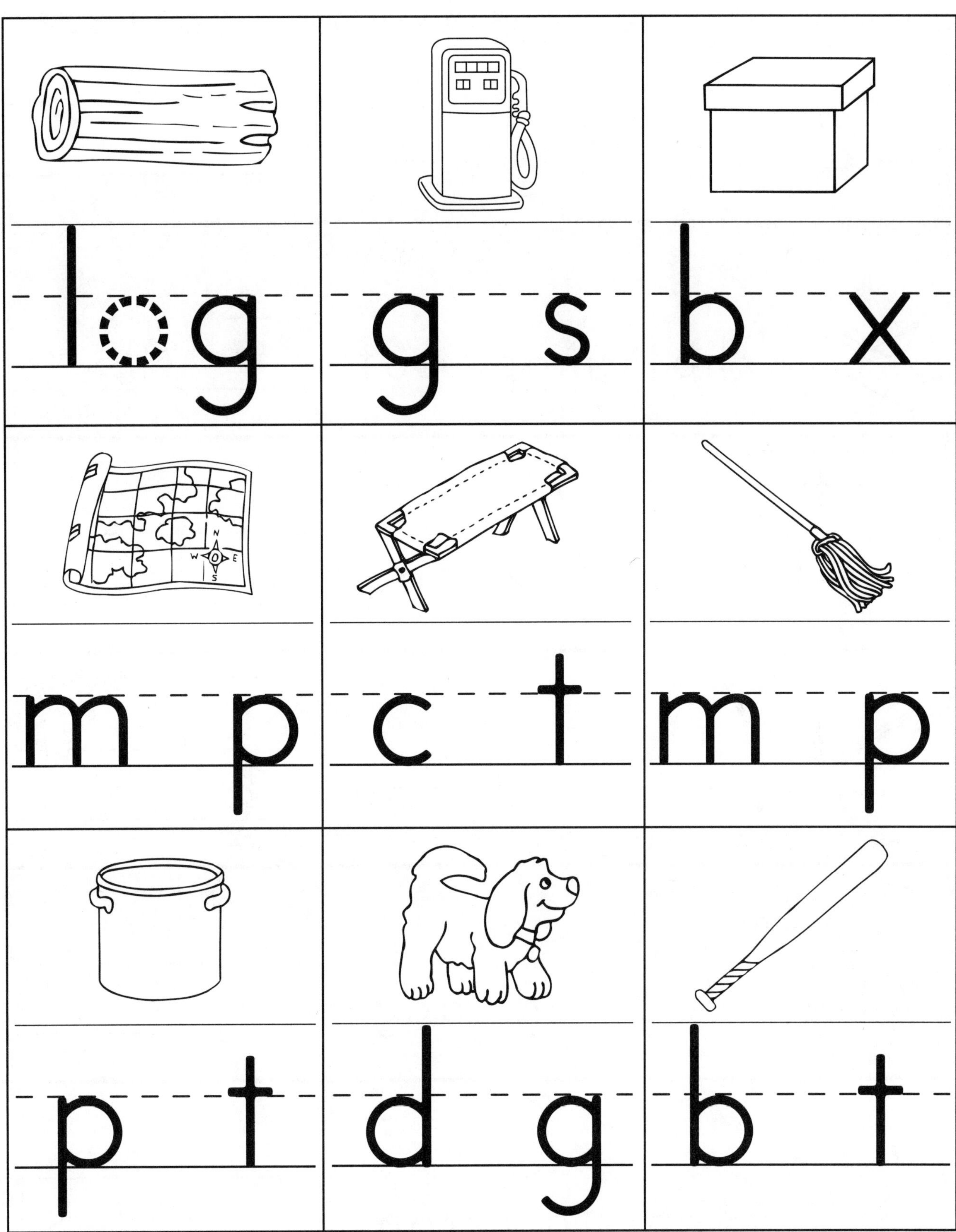

Completing Short o Words Write *o* to complete each word whose name has the short *o* sound.

Name

p

o

t

hot mop cot

box fox fog

mat rod nod

dog log bag

tap tag top

Recognizing Short o Words Write the word on the line that completes each sentence.

Name ______________________________

A fox is on the ____________.

pot log

The dog is on the ____________.

box cot

Don can ____________.

hop top

Tom got a ____________.

job mop

Completing Short o Sentences Write the word on the line that completes each sentence.

Name

I i

ink

I i

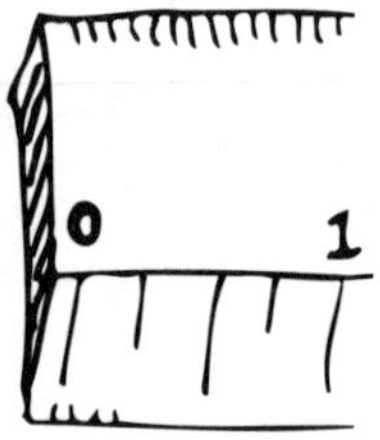

0 1

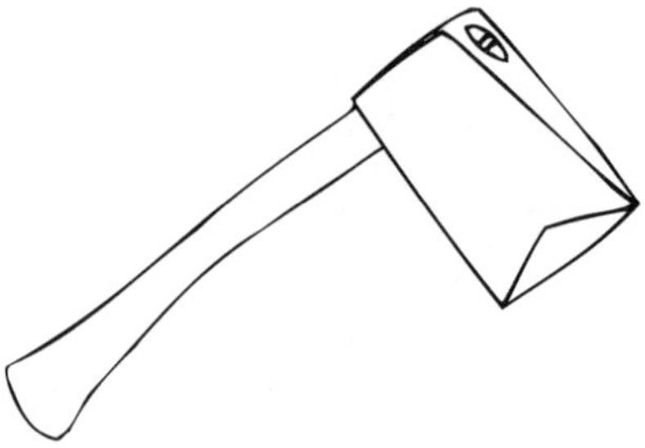

Initial Short i Trace and write the letters. Color the pictures whose names begin with the short *i* sound.

Name

Medial Short i Color the pictures whose names have the short *i* sound.

Name ____________________

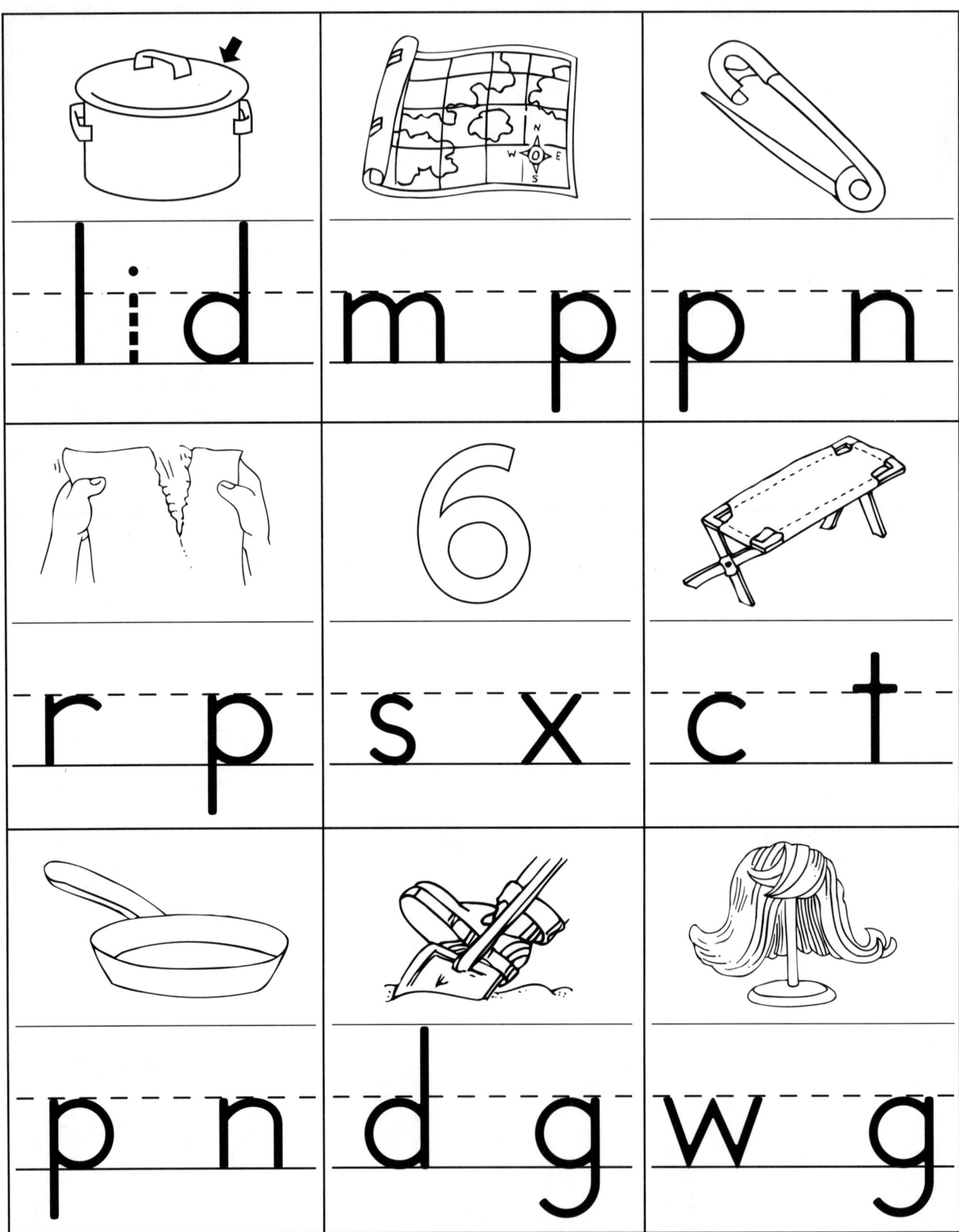

Completing Short i Words Write *i* to complete each word whose name has the short *i* sound.

Name

s i x

rib wig pit

big sit bib

pin pan win

log lad lid

pot pig pan

Recognizing Short i Words Blend and write the first word. Then circle the word that names each picture, and write it on the line.

Name

The pig can ______.

rip dig

Kim can ______.

win sip

Sid got a ______.

bib mitt

The wig is ______.

big rib

Completing Short i Sentences Write the word on the line that completes each sentence.

Name

Initial Short u Trace and write the letters. Color the pictures whose names begin with the short *u* sound.

Name ____________________

Medial Short u Color the pictures whose names have the short *u* sound.

Name ______________________

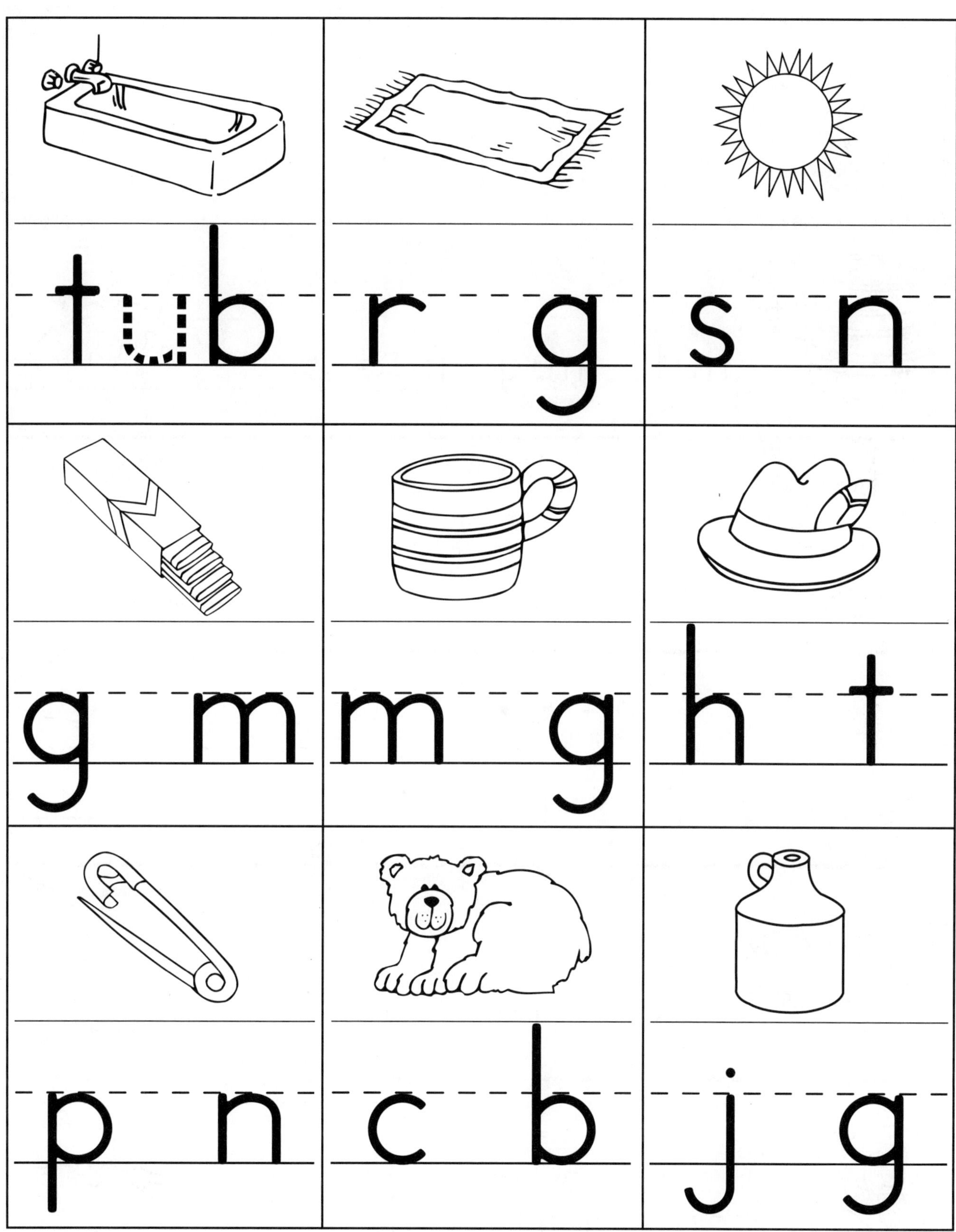

Completing Short u Words Write *u* to complete each word whose name has the short *u* sound.

Name

t

u

b

nut mug rug

sun fan bun

rib cap cup

dog bus big

cap cot cub

Recognizing Short u Words Blend and write the first word. Then circle the word that names each picture, and write it on the line.

Name ______________________

The cub is in the ______________.

bus tub

The pup is on a ______________.

rug cup

The bug is on a ______________.

jug sun

The pig has fun in ______________.

hug mud

Completing Short u Sentences Write the word on the line that completes each sentence.

Name

Ee

elephant

Initial Short e Trace and write the letters. Color the pictures whose names begin with the short *e* sound.

Name ______________________________

e 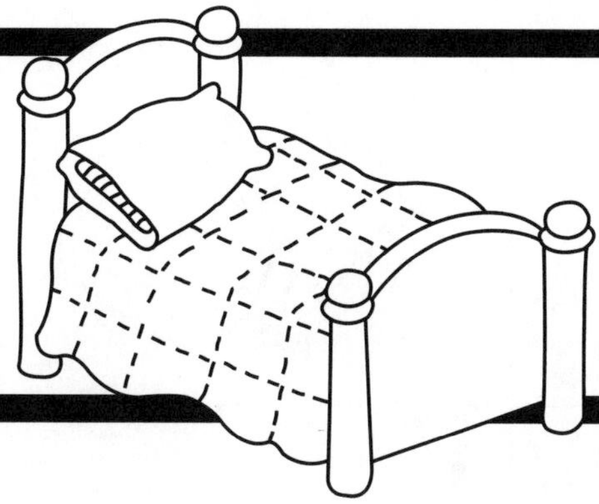 bed

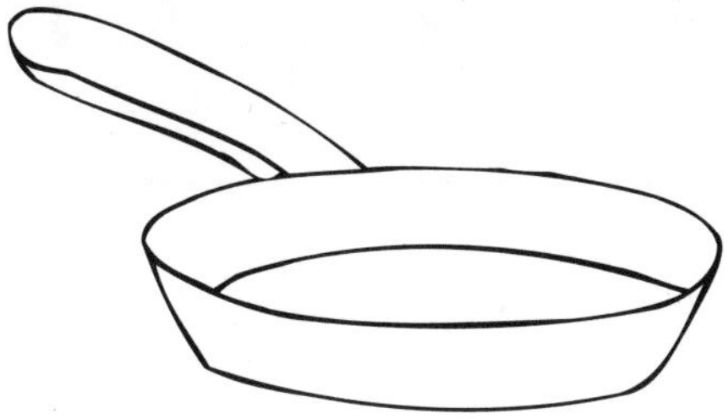

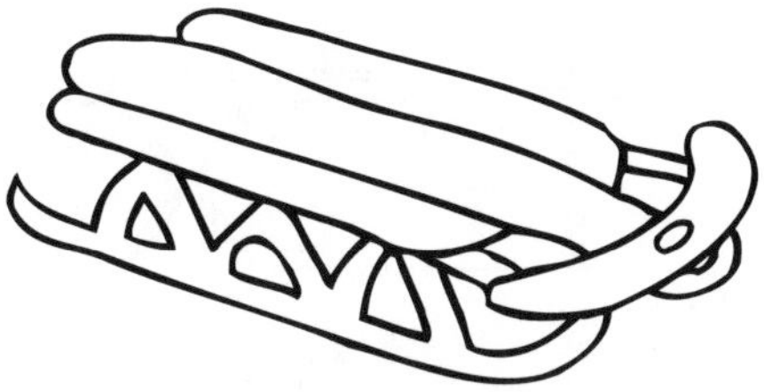

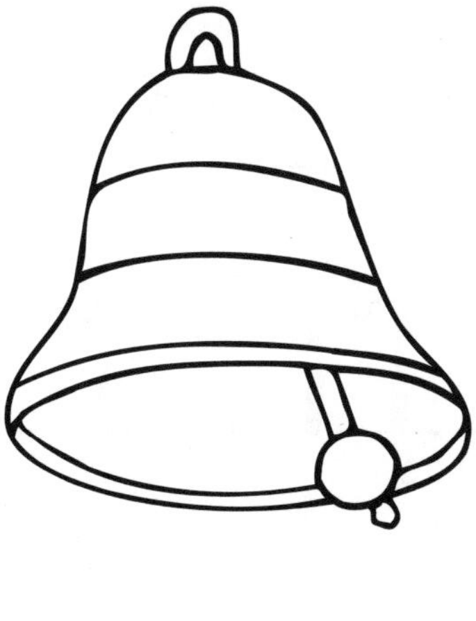

Medial Short e Color the pictures whose names have the short *e* sound.

Name

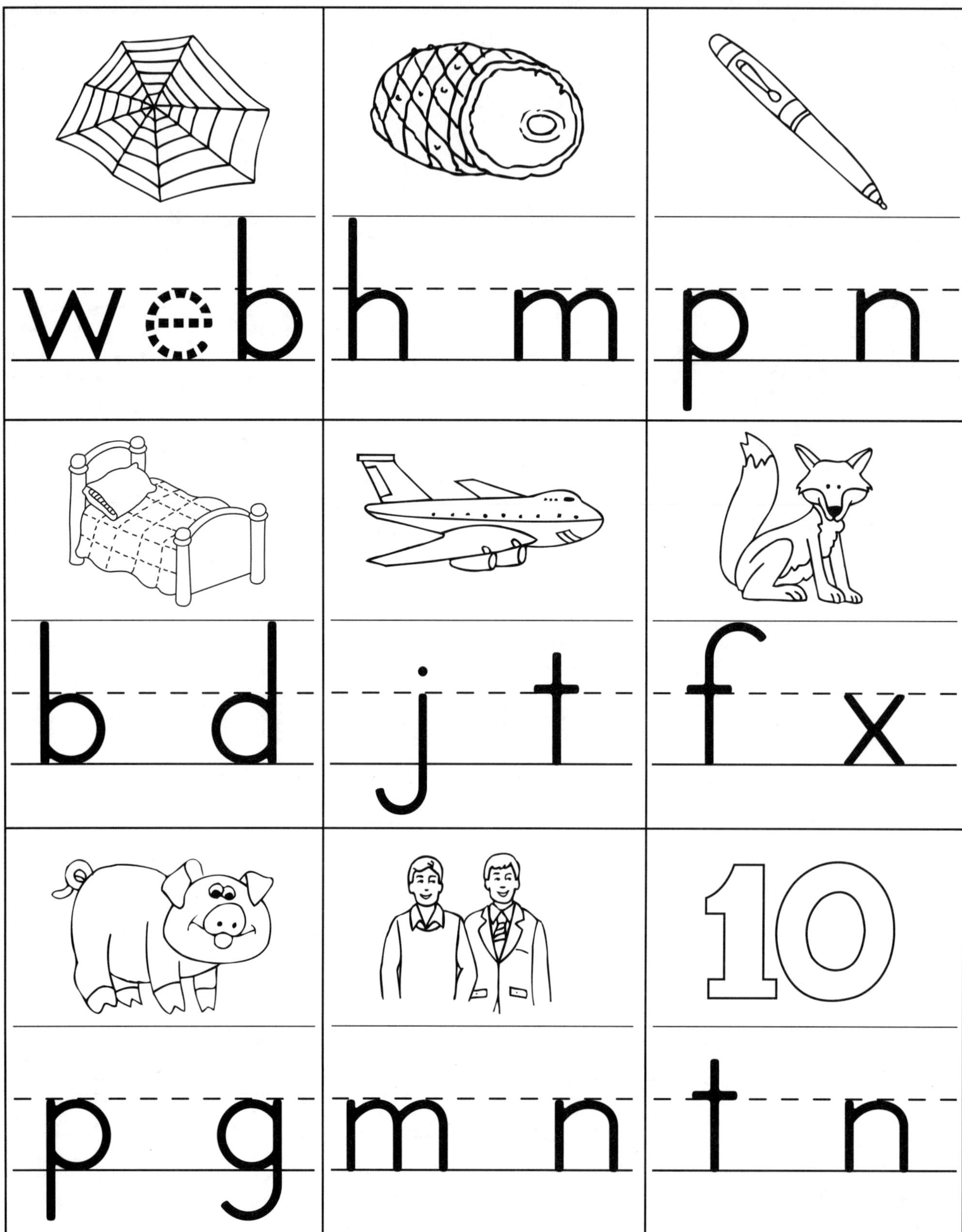

Completing Short e Words Write *e* to complete each word whose name has the short *e* sound.

Name

t e n

wet jet pit

pen net ten

not web set

net mat nut

bad big bed

Recognizing Short e Words Blend and write the first word. Then circle the word that names each picture, and write it on the line.

Name

Ben has a wet ______.

web leg

The men get on a ______.

jet bed

A red bug is in the ______.

net pen

A pet will get ______.

fed hen

Completing Short e Sentences Write the word on the line that completes each sentence.

Name

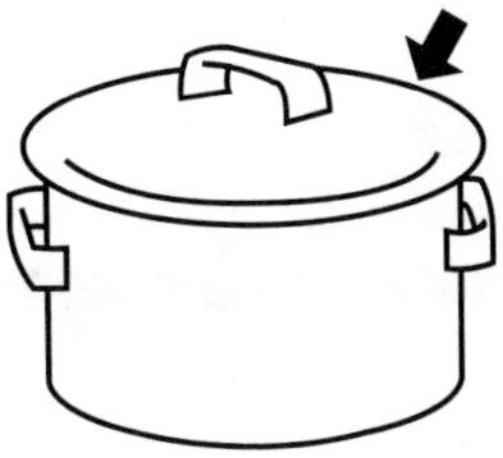 e i u	 u e a	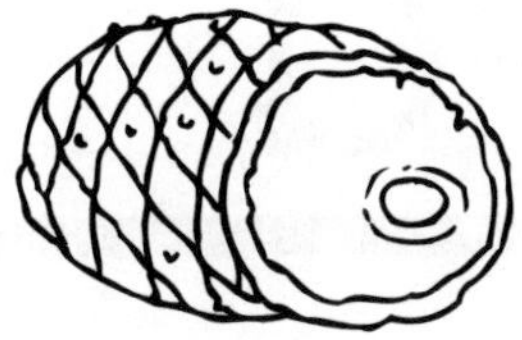 u a i
 a o u	 o a i	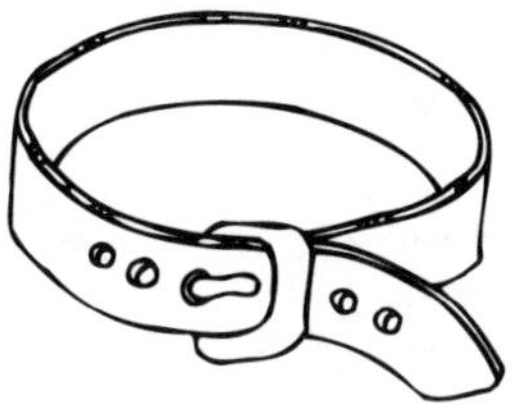 i e u
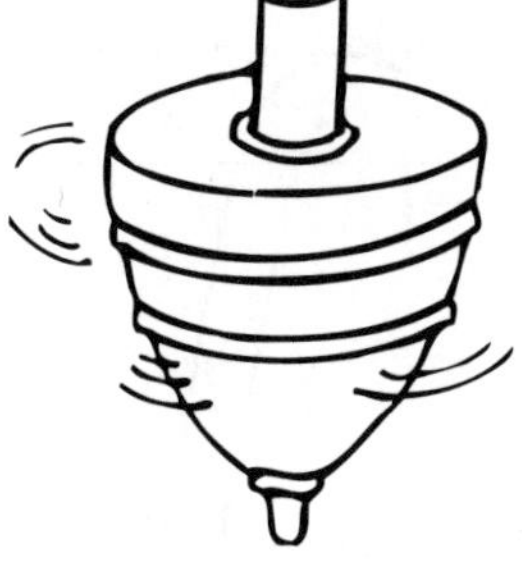 a o e	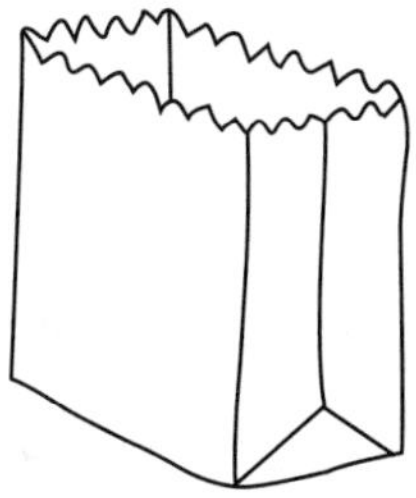 e u a	 i u a

Reviewing Short Vowel Sounds Circle and write the letter that stands for the short vowel sound in each picture name.

Name

Long a (cvce) Color the pictures whose names have the long *a* sound.

Name ______________________

Completing Long a Words (cvce) Write *a_e* to complete each word whose name has the long *a* sound.

Name ______________________________

Long a (ai) Color the pictures whose names have the long *a* sound.

Name

Completing Long a Words (ai) Write *ai* to complete each word whose name has the long *a* sound.

Name

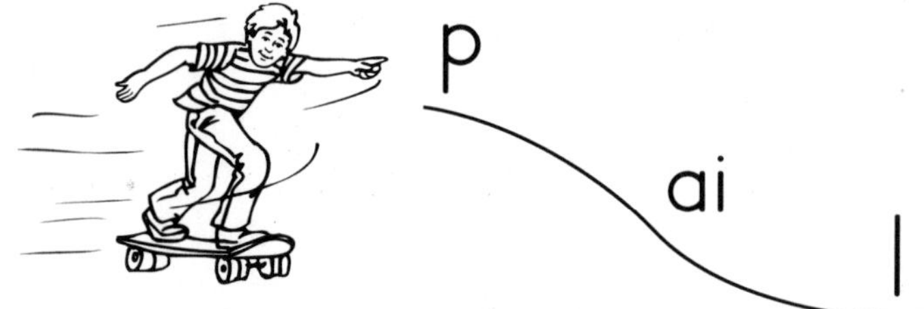

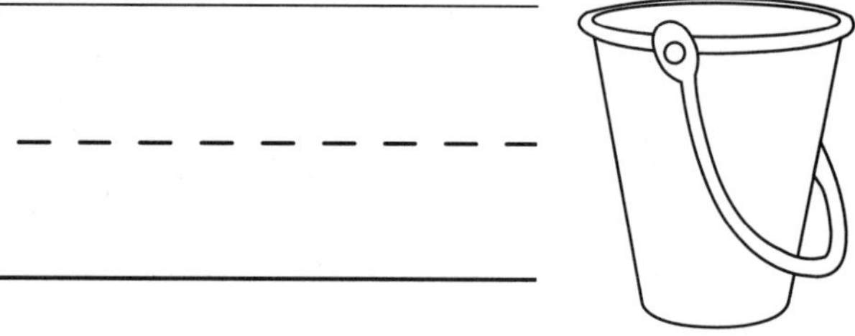

tape

tag

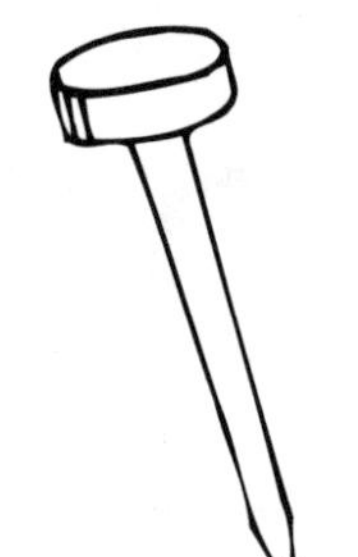

nail

nap

tab

tail

lake

lap

rat

rake

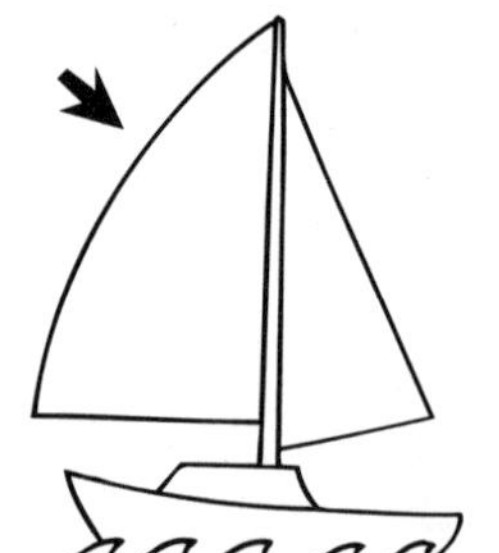

sat

sail

sat

safe

cake

cat

Recognizing Long a Words Blend and write the first word. Then circle the word that names each picture.

Name

Jane bakes a ______.

can cake

Jane takes it to the ______.

lake lap

The cake is in the ______.

ran rain

Jane saves it with a ______.

pail pad

Completing Long a Sentences Write the word on the line that completes each sentence.

Name

i

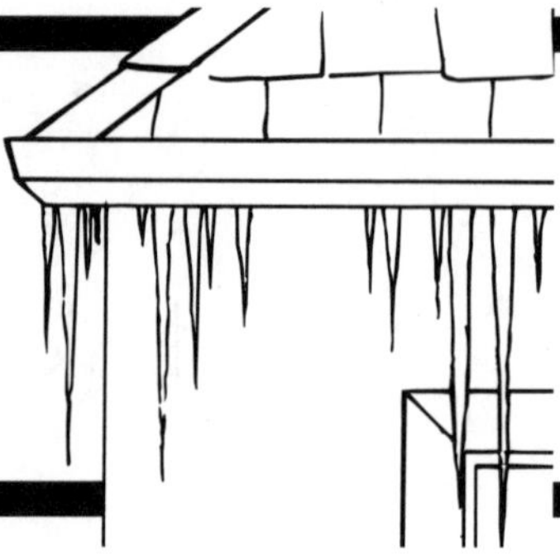

ice

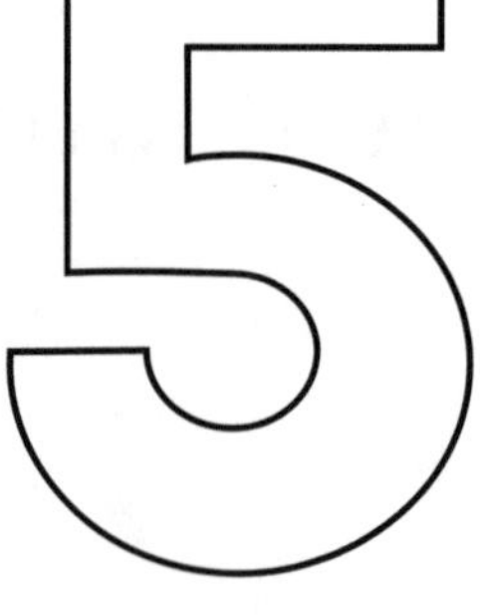

Long i (cvce) Color the pictures whose names have the long *i* sound.

Name

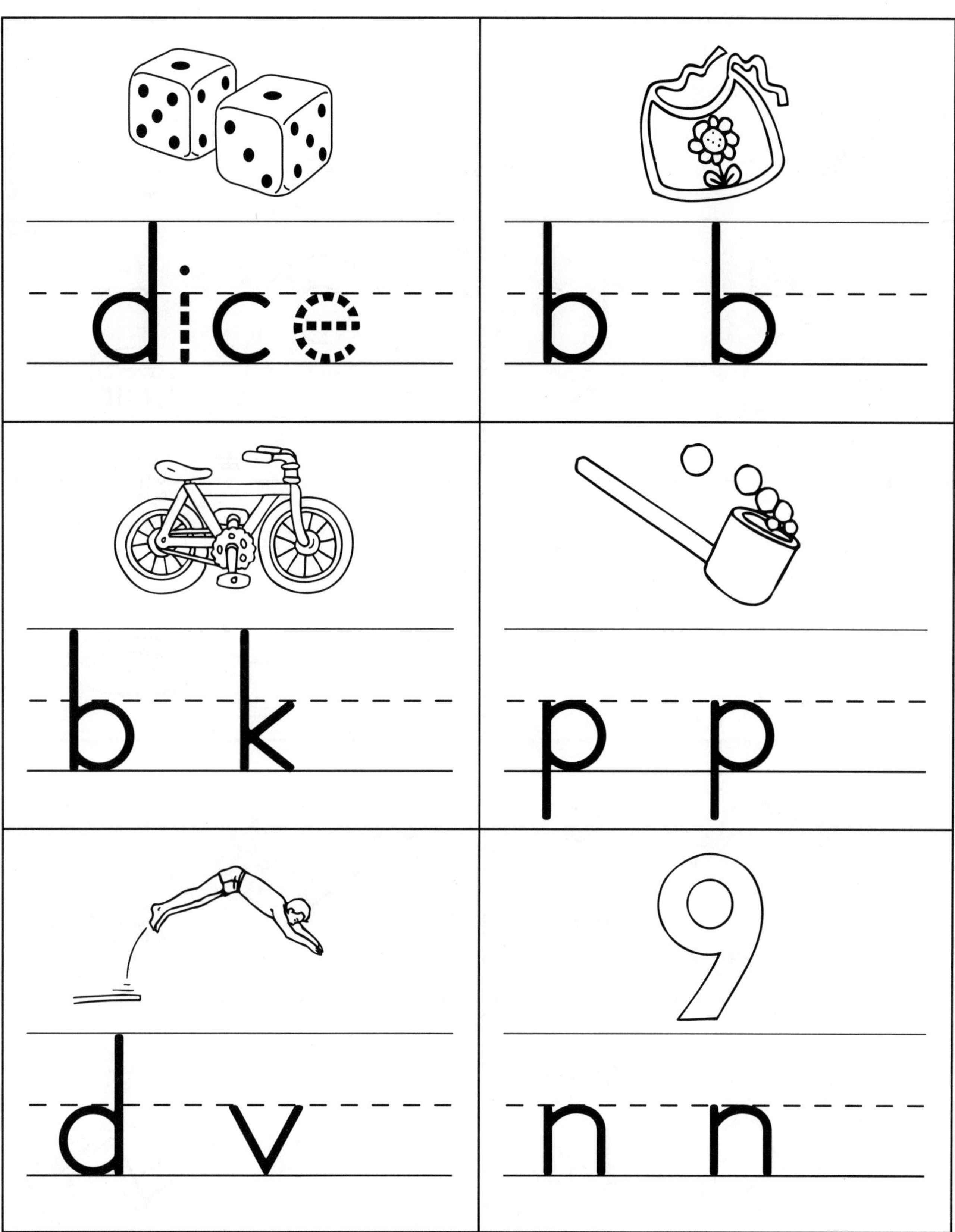

Completing Long i Words (cvce) Write *i_e* to complete each word whose name has the long *i* sound.

Name

m

i

ce

5

five

fin

nine

nip

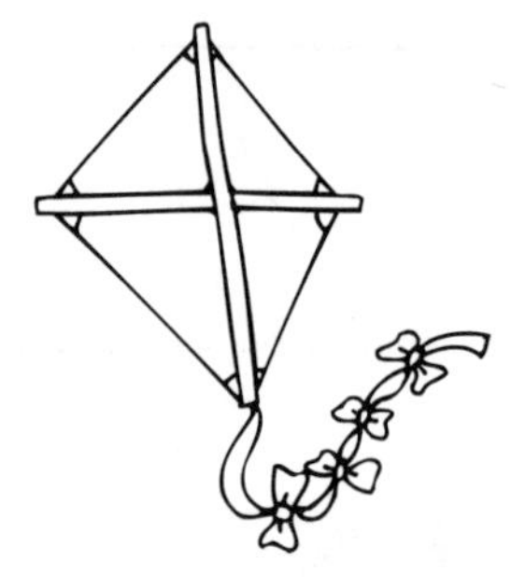

kite

kid

bit

bike

dig

dive

pipe

pin

dime

dig

win

vine

Recognizing Long i Words Blend and write the first word. Then circle the word that names each picture.

Name

Mike has a fine ______.

kite kit

The kite is up in a ______.

pin pine

Mike got it with a ______.

line lid

He put the kite on a ______.

bib bike

Completing Long i Sentences Write the word on the line that completes each sentence.

Name ______________________________

Long o (cvce) Color the pictures whose names have the long *o* sound.

Name

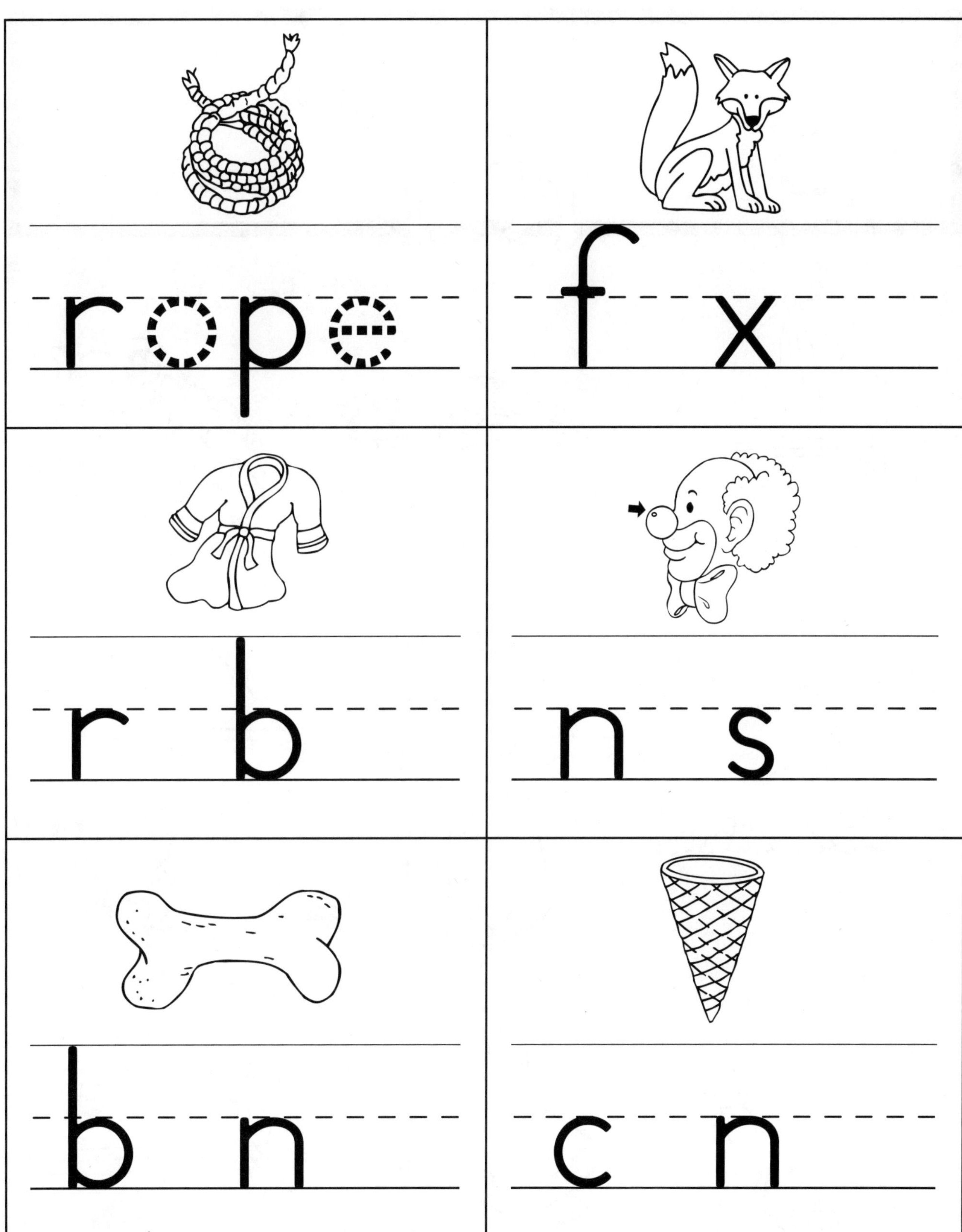

Completing Long o Words (cvce) Write *o_e* to complete each word whose name has the long *o* sound.

Name ______________________

Long o (oa) Color the pictures whose names have the long *o* sound.

Name ______________________

Completing Long o Words (oa) Write *oa* to complete each word whose name has the long *o* sound.

Name

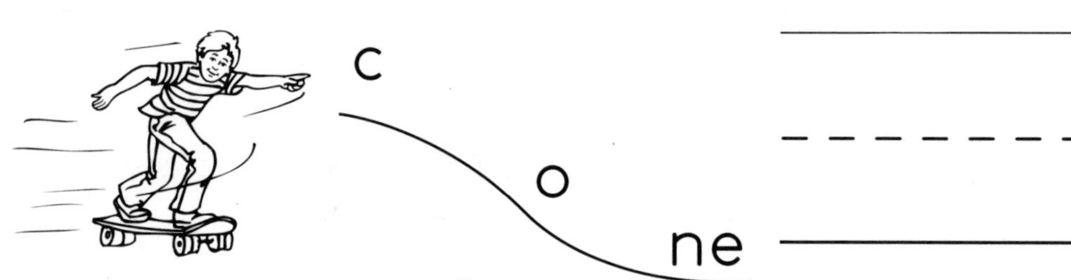

rob

road

toad

top

hop

hose

box

boat

got

goat

coat

cot

rod

robe

rose

rod

Recognizing Long o Words Blend and write the first word. Then circle the word that names each picture.

Name ______________________

A dog has a big ________.

box bone

It digs in the ________.

hole hog

A ________ pokes its nose.

top toad

The hole is its ________.

hop home

Completing Long o Sentences Write the word on the line that completes each sentence.

Name ______________________________

Long u (cvce) Color the pictures whose names have the long *u* sound.

Name ______________________

Completing Long u Words (cvce) Write *u_e* to complete each word whose name has the long *u* sound.

Name ______________________________

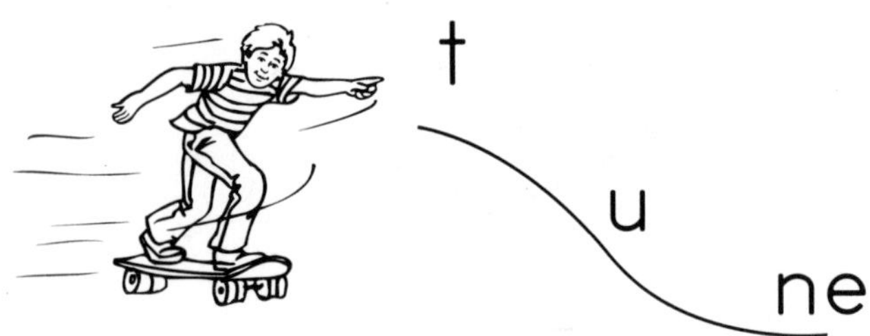

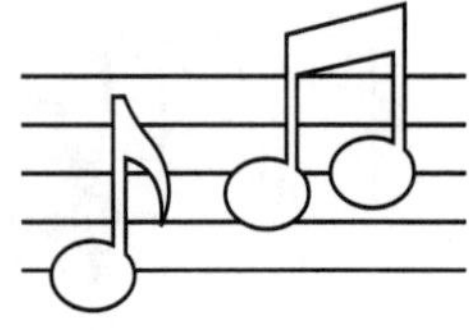

mud

mule

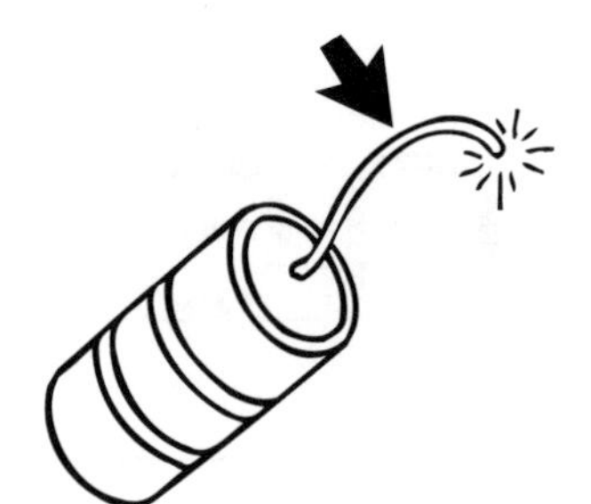

fun

fuse

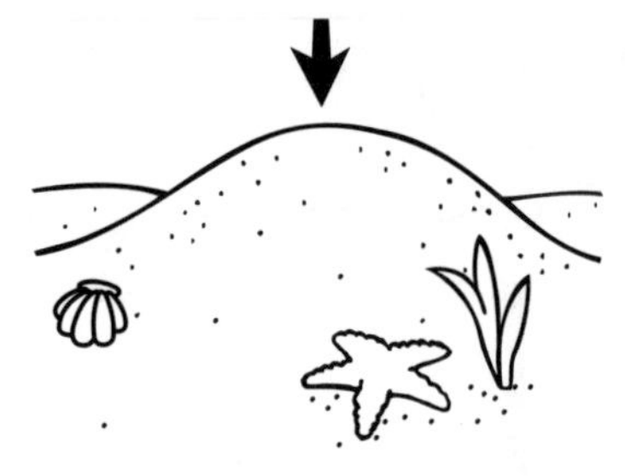

dune

dug

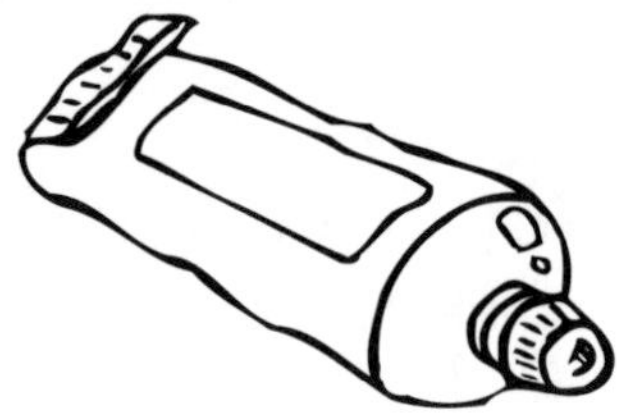

tug

tube

jug

June

huge

hum

cube

cut

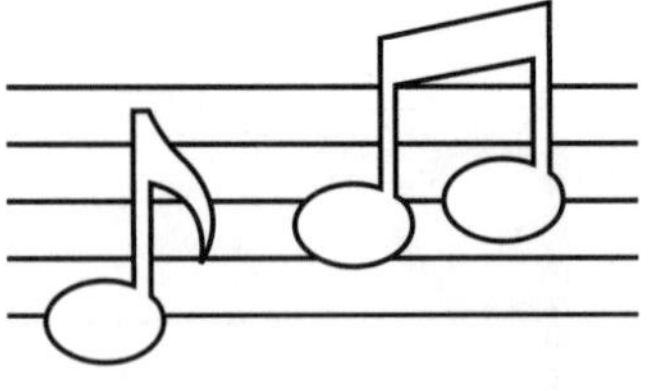

tub

tune

Recognizing Long u Words Blend and write the first word. Then circle the word that names each picture.

Name ______________________

June has a ______ pal.

cut cute

Luke has a big ______.

mule mud

They see a ______ fair.

hug huge

The mule gets a ______.

cube cub

Completing Long u Sentences Write the word on the line that completes each sentence.

Name

Long e (ee) Color the pictures whose names have the long *e* sound.

Name

Completing Long e Words (ee) Write *ee* to comlete each word whose name has the long *e* sound.

Name ______________________

Long e (ea) Color the pictures whose names have the long *e* sound.

Name

Completing Long e Words (ea) Write *ea* to complete each word whose name has the long *e* sound.

Name

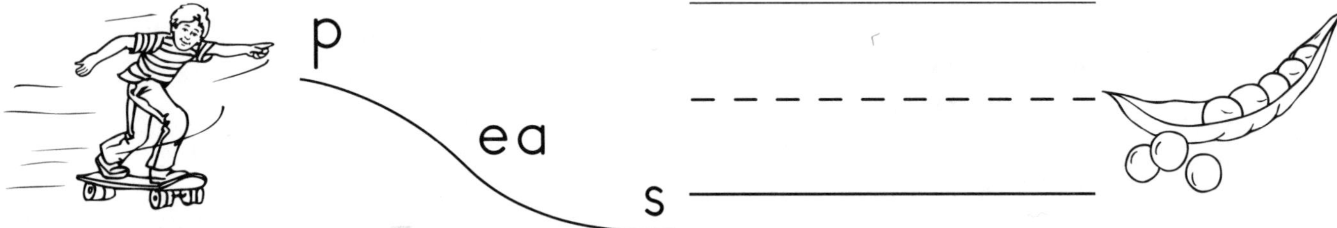

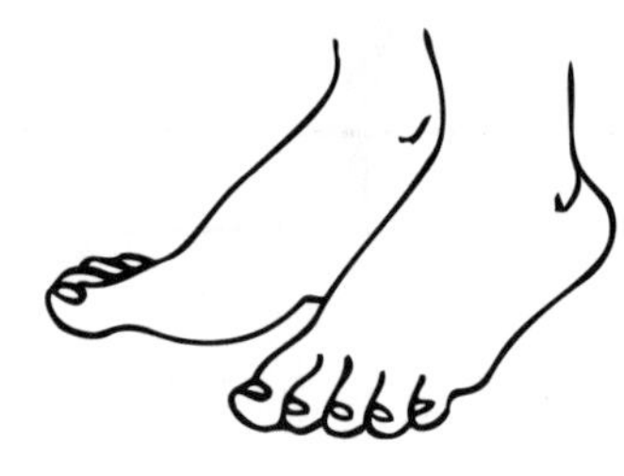

fed

feet

leaf

leg

seal

set

jet

jeep

men

meat

beak

bed

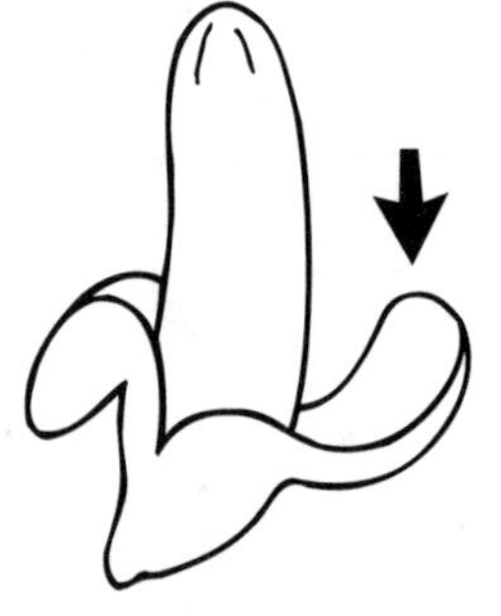

pet

peel

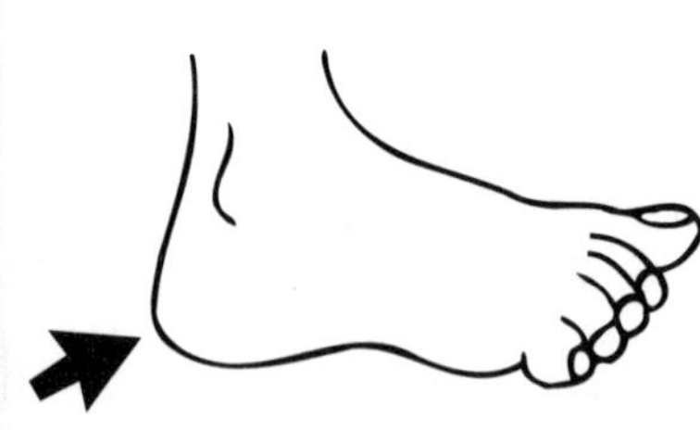

hen

heel

Recognizing Long e Words Blend and write the first word. Then circle the word that names each picture.

Name

The team will eat a __________.

meal men

Lee will take __________.

men meat

Bea will like the __________.

beet bed

The team will __________ fine.

fun feel

Completing Long e Sentences Write the word on the line that completes each sentence.

Name ______________________________

 e i o	 u a i	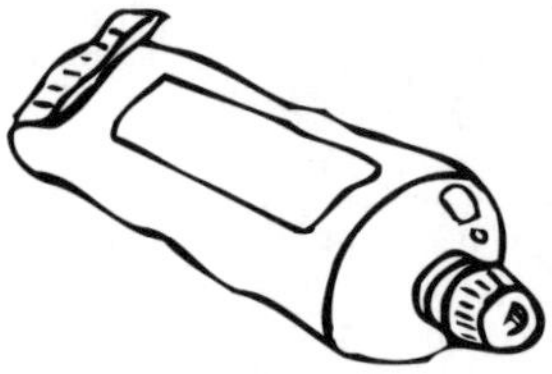 o e u
 e u o	 a e u	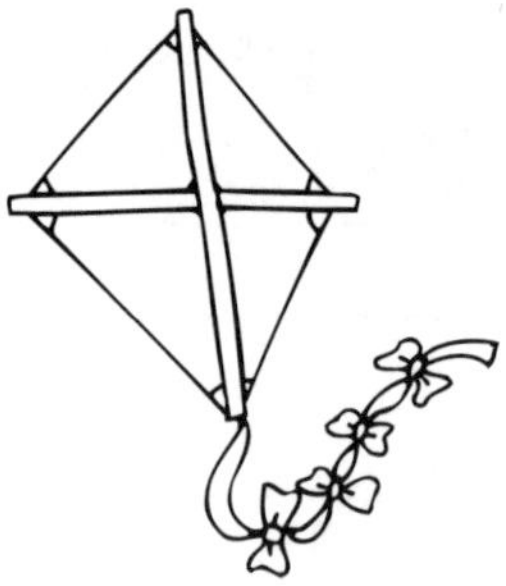 o e i
 i o a	 u e i	 e o u

Reviewing Long Vowel Sounds Circle the letter that stands for the long vowel sound in each picture name.

Name ______________________

Reviewing Vowel Sounds Circle the word that names each picture.

Name

Kate rides in the ______.

run rain

A bug is on a ______.

net note

Meg fell in the ______.

mule mud

The hen eats a ______.

seed sock

Reviewing Vowel Sounds Write the word on the line that completes each sentence.

TONGUE TWISTERS

SHORT VOWELS

Short a
An actor asked an actress about adding additional actors in the act about ants in the attic.

Short e
Extra elephants entered the elevator exactly at eleven and elbowed everybody else out.

Short i
An important inventor invented important ink and immediately invited important inventors in.

Short o
An odd octopus often offers olives to officers in offices.

Short u
Uncle Umbert is unhappy unless under his umbrella during unusual weather.

LONG VOWELS

Long a
Abe aids the ape with the aching ankle.

Long e
Electric eels elect equal teams in each event.

Long i
I like ice and ice cream on the icy island.

Long o
The ogre occasionally wears old overalls at the ocean.

Long u
Unicorns are usually unique users of useless utensils.

ANSWER KEY

p. 4 leg, e; six, i; pot, o; gas, a; bug, u; pig, i; log, o; hat, a; bed, e

p. 5 dime, i; rope, o; game, a; mule, u; vase, a; queen, e; leaf, e; bike, i; coat, o

p. 8 ax, anchor, apple, alligator, astronaut

p. 9 ham, jam, fan, can, gas, bat

p. 10 ham, cat, pan, cap, bag, mat

p. 11 pan, bag, ham, map, fan, hat

p. 12 bag, man, map, cap

p. 13 ostrich, olives, otter, ox

p. 14 box, mop, doll, cot, sock, top

p. 15 log, box, cot, mop, pot, dog

p. 16 pot, cot, box, rod, dog, top

p. 17 log, cot, hop, job

p. 18 insects, inch, igloo, ill

p. 19 six, fish, wig, bib, pig, lid

p. 20 lid, pin, rip, six, dig, wig

p. 21 six, wig, bib, pin, lid, pig

p. 22 dig, win, mitt, big

p. 23 up, umpire, untie, under

p. 24 drum, bus, cub, jug, brush, plug, duck

p. 25 tub, rug, sun, gum, mug, cub, jug

p. 26 tub, mug, sun, cup, bus, cub

p. 27 tub, rug, jug, mud

p. 28 elbow, elevator, egg, elf, exit

p. 29 web, dress, sled, nest, bell, desk

p. 30 web, pen, bed, jet, men, ten

p. 31 ten, jet, pen, web, net, bed

p. 32 leg, jet, net, fed

p. 33 lid, i; sun, u; ham, a; drum, u; mop, o; belt, e; top, o; bag, a; fish, i

p. 34 cape, vase, safe, tape, game, cake, cane

p. 35 wave, lake, gate, vase, cane

p. 36 sail, mail, nail, tail, rain

p. 37 rain, sail, pail, mail, nail

p. 38 pail, tape, nail, tail, lake, rake, sail, safe, cake

p. 39 cake, lake, rain, pail

p. 40 mice, bike, dime, vine, dice, five, pipe

p. 41 dice, bike, pipe, dive, nine

p. 42 mice, five, nine, kite, bike, dive, pipe, dime, vine

p. 43 kite, pine, line, bike

p. 44 rose, rope, cone, nose, robe, hose

p. 45 rope, robe, nose, bone, cone

p. 46 boat, toad, road, coat, soap

p. 47 soap, toad, coat, boat, goat

p. 48 cone, road, toad, hose, boat, goat, coat, robe, rose

p. 49 bone, hole, toad, home

p. 50 mule, flute, tube, fuse, June, dune

p. 51 tune, tube, mule, cube, fuse

p. 52 tune, mule, fuse, dune, tube, June, huge, cube, tune

p. 53 cute, mule, huge, cube

p. 54 queen, beet, jeep, wheel, feet, sheep

p. 55 heel, peel, feet, seed, jeep

p. 56 seal, beak, bean, meat, tea, peas

p. 57 beak, leaf, meat, peas, seal

p. 58 peas, feet, leaf, seal, jeep, meat, beak, peel, heel

p. 59 meal, meat, beet, feel

p. 60 boat, o; cake, a; tube, u; seal, e; nail, a; kite, i; hose, o; sheep, e; flute, u

p. 61 pipe, cube, sun, jet, man, lake, box, robe, pin, heel

p. 62 rain, net, mud, seed